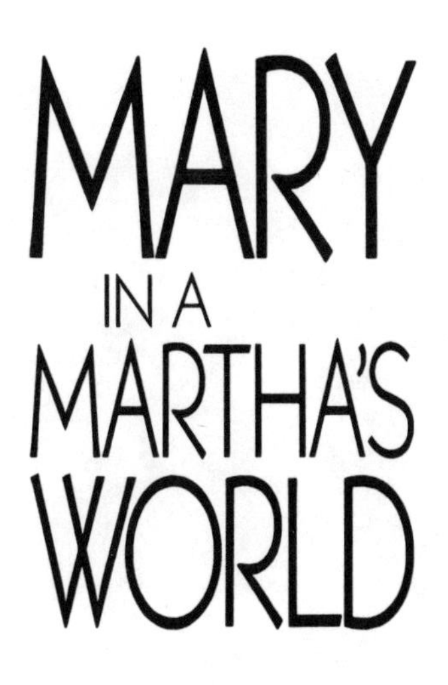
MARY
IN A
MARTHA'S
WORLD

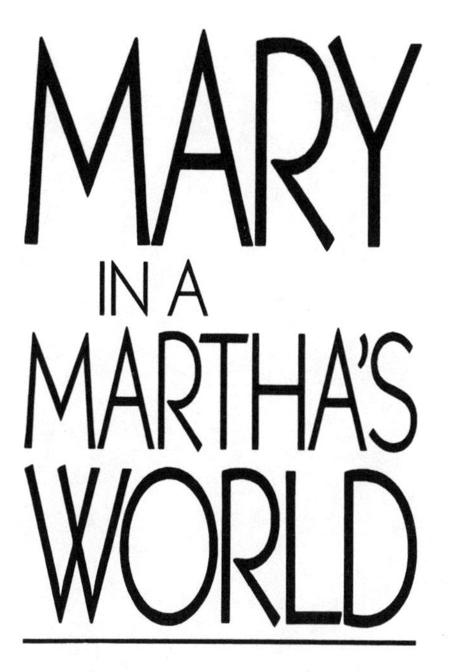

MARY IN A MARTHA'S WORLD

Quiet Times for Busy Mothers

Rita Schweitz

AUGSBURG • Minneapolis

MARY IN A MARTHA'S WORLD
Quiet Times for Busy Mothers

Illustrations by Marc Harrison.

Library of Congress Cataloging-in-Publication Data

Schweitz, Rita, 1956–
Mary in a Martha's world : quiet times for busy mothers / Rita Schweitz.
p. cm.
ISBN 0-8066-2410-8
1. Mothers—Prayer-books and devotions—English. I. Title.
BV4847.S38 1989
242'.6413—dc19 89-6511
CIP

Manufactured in the U.S.A. AF 9-2410

1 2 3 4 5 6 7 8 9 0 1 2 3 4 5 6 7 8 9

Dedicated with love
to the special kids
who have made me a
busy and happy mother:

Erin Joie
Martha Renae
Cale Thomas
Evan Michael

Contents

Acknowledgments

The quote on page 20 by Edith Schaeffer is from *What Is a Family?* © 1982 Fleming H. Revell Company. Used by permission.

The quotes on page 21 by Warren Wiersbe are reprinted by permission from *Confident Living*, copyright © 1988 by the Good News Broadcasting Association, Inc.

The quote on page 22 by Tim Kimmel is from the book *Little House on the Freeway*, copyright 1987 by Tim Kimmel, published by Multnomah Press, Portland, Oregon, 97266. Used by permission.

The quote on page 55 by Calvin Miller is taken from *The Table of Inwardness* by Calvin Miller. © 1984 by InterVarsity Christian Fellowship and used by permission of InterVarsity Press.

The quote on page 76 by Hannah Whitall Smith is from *The Christian's Secret of a Happy Life* © 1952 Fleming H. Revell Company. Used by permission.

The quote on pages 74-75 by James Dobson is from *Emotions, Can You Trust Them?* by James Dobson. © Copyright 1980, Regal Books, Ventura, CA 93006. Used by permission.

The quote on page 112 by Barbara Rainey is from "Straight Talk to Wives," *World Challenge*, March/April 1988, © 1988 Campus Crusade for Christ.

The quotes on pages 125-126 by Sue Monk Kidd are from *God's Joyful Surprise: Finding Yourself Loved.* Copyright © 1987 by Guideposts Associates Inc. Reprinted by permission of Harper & Row, Publishers, Inc.

“As Jesus and his disciples were on their way, he came to a village where a woman named Martha opened her home to him. She had a sister called Mary, who sat at the Lord’s feet listening to what he said. But Martha was distracted by all the preparations that had to be made. She came to him and asked, ‘Lord, don’t you care that my sister has left me to do the work by myself? Tell her to help me!’

‘Martha, Martha,’ the Lord answered, ‘you are worried and upset about many things, but only one thing is needed. Mary has chosen what is better, and it will not be taken away from her.’”

Luke 10:38-42

Preface

Somewhere inside every believer is a "Mary." The Mary in us hungers for meaning in life and thirsts for God's personal attention. She calls us to quiet conversation at the feet of Jesus. She is the person inside our deepest selves who is dissatisfied with any activity that crowds intimacy out of our lives. Mary beckons us to slow down, to love lavishly.

But we live in a world geared for "Marthas." Doers, who are practical and preoccupied with meeting the needs at hand, fit in well. Those who choose to take time for solitude, silence, and prayer may feel like misfits. Our noisy, hurried, hassled life-styles resist simplicity and rebel at the idea that we may not be choosing the best part.

If we are to come to Christ, it must be in the midst of a world that opposes our inner movement toward him. We must "reach out for him and find him, though he is not far from each one of us. For in him we live and move and have our being" (Acts 17:27-28). God is not absent, even in a world too busy to notice God's presence. In the midst of a "Martha's world," God will make himself heard if we, like Mary, will listen!

The Children God Has Graciously Given

"*Then Esau looked up and saw the women and children. 'Who are these with you?' he asked. Jacob answered, 'They are the children God has graciously given. . . .'*

Genesis 33:5

Walking through and around the toys and puzzle pieces that littered the carpet, I went from room to room, pausing in each one to scan the counters. I could identify with the children of Israel, who wandered 40 years in search of the promised land (a rather large item to misplace). Who's to say it wouldn't take that long to locate my Bible?

Our four little children—one still teetering, one toddling, and two talking nonstop—were all taking naps *at the same time!* It had been weeks since I'd had my daily devotions, at least in the conventional sense. Recognizing this divine intervention on my behalf, I intended to read and pray, provided the Lord could somehow part the sea of clutter long enough for me to unearth my Bible.

Could it be in the kitchen? Looking over the aftermath of a single meal, I surmised that God could have had our kitchen in mind when he spoke of the land "flowing with milk . . . and honey." We had honey on toast for breakfast, and now anyone venturing into the kitchen will likely stick tight. No time for cleanup now—I want to read.

Like the Israelites, I have been on my feet a while, and I don't particularly care for the parade route. I long to sit down and listen to the voice of God. In fact, I'd settle for just sitting down! As for listening to a still, small voice, my ears are still ringing from small voices that are rarely still. Generally speaking, our kids are generally speaking.

Unlike the undisturbed quiet of the wilderness, our home comes equipped with 24-hour-a-day interruption potential. I am always on call. Seldom is the day when one of my "beepers" doesn't go off while I'm on the phone, in the tub, or at the brink of losing my cool.

"Where is that Bible? I wish the kids wouldn't keep pack-ratting my stuff!" I mutter as I take another lap around an untouched mountain of laundry junked on the porch floor. Like the children of Israel, I have a gift for grumbling and feeling sorry for myself. Too easily I fall in step with a world that mutters against children as if they were the eleventh plague.

Turning the corner into our bedroom, I find our two-year-old perched atop my beloved Bible, preparing to attempt a front one-and-a-half into the waterbed.

God and I chuckle. Gently I am reminded that children are indeed the blessing, not the curse. Looking over the morning, I could see how Jesus had been playing with the children. Smiling at them.

Even during our busy daily routine, God is with us. And I am to be content, enjoying God and God's four gifts to me at the same time, even if it means washing two loads of "gift wrap" a day!

■ Father, how blessed I am to enjoy such precious little people! You know how easily I lose my perspective when I'm knee-deep in toys, laundry, or crying bodies. Forgive me for grumbling about having to pick up after the kids. Who will I pick up, after they are grown? Thank you so much that my arms are full now.

MARY SAT LISTENING

Mary Sat Listening

"*Mary . . . sat at the Lord's feet listening to what he said.*

Luke 10:39

Mary sat still. She drew close to Jesus. She listened. Mary's actions show that she valued intimacy enough to take time for Jesus.

Mary was willing to take time to talk. She was willing to be her own person, seeking and serving God with an authenticity and sincerity based on firsthand knowledge of God's love for her. And she acted on her love even when family and friends objected to her "extravagance."

Mary was extravagant in her use of time to express love. She valued her relationship with Jesus and lavishly spent time with him—even when there was work to be done in his service! How often does "doing something for" supplant "being with" people as the appropriate means of expressing love, not only in respect to our interactions with Christ, but also with children, spouse, and friends?

Mary was also extravagant in her use of money to express love for Jesus (John 12:3). She used perfume that cost more than a year's wages (see Mark 14:5) in a single act of adoration! Her lavish generosity, based on caring concern for Jesus, clearly showed that she valued him as a person far above possessions or public approval.

A friendship with Jesus that is strong enough to help us overcome self-consciousness, meaningful enough to motivate us to spend time in prayer, and personal enough to prompt our giving is rare. We have often settled for the form of religion and missed the life-changing reality. We talk far more about being active than being *receptive!*

In our quiet moments, each of us hungers for meaning in life. We thirst for the love and acceptance Jesus offers. But only intimacy with God can satisfy these needs. We, like Mary, need to choose the better part; we need to be receptive to Jesus in inner fellowship. We need to devote unusual time and intensity to prayer in order to establish intimacy.

■ Lord, you have promised that if we draw near to you, you will draw near to us. You tell us that those who seek will find. I want to come close to you. I want to make time to get to know you. I want to draw near like Mary, but I'm unsure how to approach you. Please help me find the reality of a deeper relationship with you.

Created in Christ for Good Works

"*For we are God's workmanship, created in Christ Jesus to do good works, which God prepared in advance for us to do.*

Ephesians 2:10

The television commercial urges "Be all that you can be!" The media message appeals to our desire for self-fulfillment, but it implies twisted truth.

You can't be *all* that you can be: one choice often rules out another. Some pursuits are incompatible; others are mutually exclusive. You may have the talent to be a world class athlete and the opportunity to attend medical school, but the intensive hours of training needed to succeed at either force you to choose only one. Money, time, training, and family responsibilities all set perimeters on your potential.

In the story of Mary and Martha, Jesus said, "Mary has chosen what is better" (Luke 10:42). Choosing the "best part" means not choosing other things in the small decisions that crowd each day, as well as the major choices. "We are finite, and in our finiteness and limitedness we can never choose to do something without choosing not to do something else. There is usually the need to put aside ten other things to do one special thing," writes Edith Schaeffer (*What Is a Family?* Hodder & Stoughton, 1975). We can't do it all; we can't be all that we could possibly be.

"Be what only *you* can be!" is a more biblical perspective. God has given you an original set of abilities and interests. It is fascinating to think that God has prepared in advance the good works that you are uniquely created to do. And God will open up the necessary doors for you to become the person he desires you to be, beginning where you are.

How do we know which things we're supposed to do? Bible teacher Dr. Warren W. Wiersbe tells us, "They have two marks: (1) God wants you to do them, and (2) we are the only ones who can do them." He goes on to explain that Christians can pray with and seek council from one another. "But in the end, each of us must decide what God wants us to do."

Dr. Wiersbe gives an example from his own experience. "My wife and I tried to follow this principle when our children were still at home. . . . *Only we can be their parents*. More than once we have said 'no' to invitations that would have taken us away from events where nobody could adequately substitute for mom and dad."

God has prepared some things he wants you to do. You are the only one who can do them. So, be all you're meant to be!

■ Father, only I can be a wife to my husband and a mother to my children. Help me to do a good job with these assignments. And beyond that, Lord, help me choose to do the things which you desire. Don't let me grab for the gratifications of my own selfish ambitions.

Become One Flesh

"*A man will leave his father and mother and be united to his wife, and they will become one flesh.*

Genesis 2:24

Our couples' Bible study was using a book titled, *Two Become One*, which stressed building closeness in marriage. A young husband in the group, the father of three children in quick succession, noted the title and commented, "That's fine, but it *should* read *Two Become Three or Four or Five!*"

We all burst out laughing. The more prolific the pair, the louder the laughter! Everyone understood the point: it's hard to maintain "oneness" when baby makes three or five or six!

Tim Kimmel, in *Little House on the Freeway,* wrote, "Not all marriages are hurting, but it's hard to find one that isn't hassled. Hurried living does that to you. The most conscientious couple can find their commitment tested just because they have too many legitimate responsibilities competing for the time it takes to maintain a healthy marriage."

Intimacy takes time! So do children. Often it is the physical side of oneness that suffers first. Newborns, fatigue, hurried lives, and a quality sex life are incapable of existing in harmony. Adjustments must be made to avoid discord.

The average couple has access to ample information on marriage to know what these adjustments are. They know they should make time for talking and togetherness, make marriage a high priority, make sure the emotional and sexual needs of each spouse are met. But they don't do it!

As wives and mothers we need to ask ourselves: Does

my husband ever get my undivided attention, or am I always preoccupied or talking? Do I respect my husband? Am I making sure the children and my work don't consume all my energies and attention?

At a retreat, the speaker was suggesting that every mother occasionally get a sitter in order to have some time alone with her husband. She closed with the comment, "Anyone can take care of your kids. Only *you* can take care of your husband!"

■ Father, I really desire the oneness the Bible describes. But it's so easy to let everything else crowd out our time together. Teach me how to protect that time in our schedule. Help me balance the many responsibilities that compete for the time it takes to achieve true unity.

Careful to Discipline

"*He who spares the rod hates his son, but he who loves him is careful to discipline him.*

Proverbs 13:24

Billy Graham tells the story of a Christian mother who received this advice concerning her young son, "All the boy needs is a pat on the back."

"Yes," she replied, "if it's low enough and hard enough!"

Regulating the proper blend of praise and discipline isn't always easy. It's tough to fairly and calmly discipline our children. And it can be hard to encourage and praise them frequently. But the Bible teaches that we should consistently do both.

On the one hand, it is possible to allow a child's "sense of sinfulness to grow out of all proportion to his sense of self-worth," to use a Calvin Miller phrase. As those in authority, we may begin to coerce the child's behavior rather than correct it. On the other hand, it is possible to cripple a child with excessive praise and tolerance, failing to teach him or her self-discipline or self-control. The child who habitually gets his or her own way will not fare well in a world that will not devote itself to fulfilling the child's desires. But between both extremes lies the heart of the matter—love.

If we love our children, we will seek a balance. We will be careful to discipline and train them. And we will be careful to encourage and esteem them. We will be faithful to lovingly administer a pat on the back, or a little lower, as needed!

■ Father, help me love my children as you love me. Make me more consistent and calm when disciplining them; more enthusiastic and eager to encourage them. Keep me careful to balance praise that encourages growth with discipline that discourages sin.

I Am the Way

"*Jesus answered, 'I am the way and the truth and the life. No one comes to the Father except through me.'*

John 14:6

A free-spirited young man was invited to attend a home Bible study. "I'm not sure I want to be around all that 'Jesus only' stuff. There are many roads to the top of the mountain, ya know!" he replied.

The man's comment showed great tolerance for a variety of philosophies and religions. He believed there are many ways to come to God. Was he right?

Many people argue that there are other ways to God. They maintain that it is not *what* you believe but *how sincerely you believe it* that matters. Their argument is not with Christians, but with Christ.

Some people see Jesus as one who puts limits on their lives. They think he said, "You have to be good and do everything my way." They imagine him to be intolerant and exclusive in his affections. To them "Jesus only" is an extreme position.

The Bible describes a different Jesus—the real one! It tells of a Jesus who is love, who died to save us. The Jesus of the Bible is unique; "Salvation is found in no one else, for there is no other name under heaven given to men by which we must be saved" (Acts 4:12).

Why Jesus only? Because Jesus is the only begotten Son of God, sent by God to conquer death. Only Jesus loved us enough to sacrifice himself for our sins! Jesus *is* "the way and the truth and the life." We can believe him!

There aren't many roads to God. "Small is the gate and narrow the road that leads to life, and only a few find it" (Matt. 7:14). Not all roads lead to the top of the mountain. Some roads lead to the depths of despair. And God cared enough to warn us. You can take God's word for it, or you can believe what people say.

■ Lord God, if what you say is true, it's true whether I believe it or not. And it's true for everyone, not just me. Thank you for explaining that Jesus is the way to you, so that I could believe in him. I couldn't find the way if you didn't teach me your path.

THE BETTER PART

The Better Part

“*‘Mary has chosen what is better, and it will not be taken from her.’*

Luke 10:42

When should we work and when should we worship? The use of our time is determined largely by personal preferences and priorities.

Martha chose to spend her time in the kitchen. That was fine. That was important. But she was annoyed when Mary did not follow suit. Martha came up to Jesus asking, “Don’t you care that my sister has left me. . . . Tell her to help me!” That was not fine!

Jesus rebuked Martha for trying to impose her choice upon Mary. He explained, “Mary has chosen the better part.” But he didn’t add, “So sit down here and listen!” I get the impression reading the story, that Martha probably returned to the kitchen, still ruffled, while Mary stayed put.

Martha was as entitled to her choice as Mary was. Choosing between something good and something better it a matter of personal decision. Jesus didn’t force Martha to choose the good part, but he did give her guidelines for choosing wisely. God will not force his priorities upon us, either. We must choose between the good and the better, work and worship, the important and the essential.

■ I often say I value prayer, Lord, but when saying comes to praying my schedule often betrays me. Help me to make the best use of my time, recognizing that time spent with you is the better part, the more essential thing. Keep me from being worried, upset, and distracted by so many nonessentials.

Do Not Fear, for I Am with You

"*Do not fear, for I am with you; do not anxiously look about you, for I am your God. I will strengthen you, surely I will help you, surely I will uphold you with My righteous right hand.*

Isaiah 41:10 NASB

The rattle of cold steel alerted us to the patient being wheeled from the recovery room to the pediatric ICU. In the eternal twilight of the unit, a tiny child looked anxiously about, her eyes wide with fear. She lay defenseless, strapped to her bed in the confusing semiconsciousness that follows heart surgery. Needles and tubes invaded every appendage. *Monitored for everything—except pain and fear,* I thought, my own body paralyzed by the sight.

The man beside me moved quickly into action. When he saw her fear he quickly rose and spoke, his voice choked with compassion. "Don't be afraid. It's OK, I'm here now. Daddy's not going to leave you. . . ."

As his voice soothed, he stretched his massive frame over the iron bed rails to cradle his fragile child. Bending around the infusion pump to draw his face down near hers, he stroked her hair back with one hand. The other hand he slid through the maze of tubes and restraints until it reached hers.

I watched as the child's hand closed tightly around the single finger he had laid across her palm. Turning to his voice, her eyes met his. A look of recognition and relief flooded her face, rinsing away the confusion and fear. She began to relax, but her eyes never left his, drawing strength and security from his very presence.

Over and over he crooned, "Don't be afraid, I'm here with you. I love you," until finally she drifted off to sleep. Only then did he let his contorted body slide back into the chair.

I knew how his back must have ached from the strain of holding a half-bent position for nearly two hours. I also knew without doubt that he would be there again for her when she awoke, because I knew something of the love which constrained him to stay by his daughter's side. I was her mother.

■ Father, if an earthly father's love could make him long so intently to comfort his child, how much more must you, as my Father in heaven, long to help me. I know you are bending over my life, aching to comfort and reassure me, waiting for me to turn to your voice. Instead of anxiously looking around, help me to fix my eyes on your face, drawing on your strength. When I am afraid, let me remember a child's faith in her daddy, and hold on to whatever I can touch of you.

Your Word Stands Firm

"Your word, O Lord, is eternal; it stands firm in the heavens. Your faithfulness continues through all generations; you established the earth, and it endures. Your laws endure to this day, for all things serve you.

Psalm 119:89-91

Martin Luther wrote, "Feelings come and feelings go and feelings are deceiving. Our surety is the Word of God; naught else is worth believing." Feelings are predictably fickle. God is predictably faithful. How much wiser it is to look to God's Word for guidance. But how much easier it is to do what we feel like doing!

The Bible is the enduring source of truth, inspiration, faith, and hope. But many have wandered from the Word in search of other pastures. Why? "Having been fed through the system—Sunday school, endless sermons, Bible school, prayer meetings, . . . I have often found it difficult to maintain a systematic and continuous reading of the Scripture. I had just enough background to make it seem unnecessary to probe much further," explained one man as he encouraged others to follow him in a return to *firsthand,* day-to-day Bible study.

Secondhand experience seldom satisfies. Yet many who claim to be biblical Christians have never even read the book; bits and pieces, maybe, but never a thorough investigation. They put themselves in a precarious and vulnerable position, capable of living only according to what they *think* the Bible teaches.

How about you? Do you depend on someone else's examination of Scripture, or on your own exposure to God's eternal truth? "Feelings come and feelings go" but God's Word is worth believing—check it out for yourself!

■ O God, help me make Bible study a priority. It's easier to let someone else do my thinking for me, but I don't want to take the easy way out. I want to have a personal understanding of who you are, and the truth you have revealed in your Word. Show me where to begin and how to keep going!

Wash Away All My Iniquity

"*Have mercy on me, O God, according to your unfailing love; according to your great compassion blot out my transgressions. Wash away all my iniquity and cleanse me from my sin. . . . Cleanse me with hyssop, and I will be clean; wash me, and I will be whiter than snow.*

Psalm 51:1-2, 7

One morning I was upstairs sorting clothes when our five-year-old yelled up urgently. "Mom! Mom! You'd better come down quick! Evan just got into the kitchen and spilled everything he saw!"

"Everything he *saw*?" The image registered in my mind, and I sprinted to the scene of the crime.

It wasn't that I was eager to clean up the mess, but in our household there is one axiom that always holds true: Messes multiply if not taken care of immediately.

It takes only common sense and a few bad experiences to convince us that this is true in the physical realm! But the maxim is also true of emotional and spiritual things. For instance, if we allow our frustrations to spill over into self-pity, and don't quickly clean up our attitude, what happens? The sour attitude begins to affect our dispositions and our work, in addition to our outlook.

And gossiping is a little like stepping in on the porch with muddy shoes—you may only take a step or two, but the person after you tracks mud all over the house!

Sin always spreads—within and without! Unfortunately, we are not always quick to set our inner house in order. And when we make a mess of a relationship, we may know it is best to set

things straight before any bitterness or hurt feelings multiply, but we still refuse to apologize immediately.

Scripture tells us that "if we confess our sins, he is faithful and just and will forgive us our sins and purify us from all unrighteousness" (1 John 1:9). The blood of Christ can cleanse our consciences. The sooner we confess the better!

God graciously lifts the stain of sin and leaves our hearts spotless. We may even find, as I did when I rushed to the kitchen, that we have avoided an even bigger problem by coming quickly. (Evan had spilled everything he saw—on the table. When I arrived, he was pouring salt on his butter-smeared tummy, eyeing the milk jug on the counter.)

My axiom—messes multiply if not taken care of immediately—has a corollary. No matter how disagreeable it is to straighten up now, things will only get worse if you don't!

■ Almighty God, there are areas that need cleaning up in my life; sins I need to confess. I have been living with them far too long, but even now I'm reluctant to repent. Forgive me, Lord. Thank you for cleansing my heart even from the wrong desire. Give me the strength to stop sinning, as I ask in Jesus' name.

JESUS LOVED MARTHA

Jesus Loved Martha

"*Now a man named Lazarus was sick. . . . So the sisters sent word to Jesus, 'Lord, the one you love is sick.' . . . Jesus loved Martha and her sister and Lazarus.*

John 11:1, 3, 5

Have you ever doubted God's love? Perhaps your doubt surfaced when you were sick or when God delayed in answering your heartfelt prayers, or when someone you loved lay dying. Watching helplessly as a loved one suffers is a difficult thing. But it's harder still if you have witnessed the healing ministry of Jesus on other occasions, as Mary and Martha had, only to have him out of town in your moment of need.

These sisters turned to Jesus for help. Their response to this crisis shows how well they understood Jesus. They both recognized and appealed to the depth of his love for their brother: "the one you love is sick." Mary and Martha acted on the premise we often question—God's love! When they sent for Jesus, they each expressed their confidence that Jesus not only could, but *would* heal Lazarus.

Martha's words to Jesus when he arrived, after the death of her brother, are of special interest to me: "I know that even now God will give you whatever you ask. . . . I know that he [Lazarus] will rise again in the resurrection at the last day. . . . I believe you are the Christ, the Son of God, who was to come into the world" (vv. 22, 24, 27). Where did she pick up such spiritual understanding and faith? I thought she was always busy in the kitchen! Apparently not.

Martha's inclination may have been toward activity and practicality, as ours often is, but she must have listened to God in the midst of her work. Or perhaps she took the time to learn from Jesus. In any case, she developed a deep and personal relationship with Christ *before* the crisis. When tragedy struck, she was prepared, she relied on Jesus, and the trial served to strengthen rather than overcome her faith.

Jesus loved Martha. And her sister. And Lazarus. Suffering and death did not indicate God's anger or disapproval. And they loved Jesus and trusted in his love, even when Lazarus was critically ill. Each expressed that love and faith through the unique personalities God had given them. Each had earlier built a friendship with Jesus in his or her own way.

What was natural for Martha wouldn't have suited Mary. Or me! But we do not need to act alike, imitating someone else's style. Jesus invites each of us into a relationship with him. We can come to him as we are, and he lovingly embraces us. And as we draw near to Jesus, we will be prepared. The knowledge of his love and power will give us the strength to meet the difficult circumstances life may offer.

■ Jesus, thank you that I can be myself. Thank you for allowing me freedom to develop my own learning style, my own way of relating to you and serving you. It's comforting to know I can walk according to your Spirit's guidance, and keep in step with your plans and purposes, without having to pretend to be someone I'm not. Remind me to deepen my relationship with you now so that I may be prepared, like Mary and Martha, to face future pressures with complete confidence in your love.

Teach Us to Number Our Days

"*Teach us to number our days aright, that we may gain a heart of wisdom.*

Psalm 90:12

Infancy, childhood, adolescence, youth—strung together on the thread of time. These fleeting jewels in our children's lives are unalterably set in place before our very eyes. The days we spend with our children pass so quickly.

Or do they? I spent a week with a fussy baby last Tuesday. It's taking forever to potty train our son. And it's been ages since my husband and I enjoyed an uninterrupted conversation in our home. Or so it seems. It's rather easy to lose perspective! I suspect these days only pass quickly in retrospect.

If we are not careful, "numbering our days" may mean counting off the days until our children are grown. But looking to the fulfillment of tomorrow will cheat us out of many precious moments today. On the other hand, we may become so preoccupied with the cleaning, cooking, and other responsibilities that accompany raising children that the precious moments of childhood slip by unnoticed or neglected.

This thought is captured in the following poem I noticed on a plaque.

Cleaning and scrubbing can
wait 'til tomorrow
For babies grow up, we've
learned to our sorrow
So quiet down, cobwebs,
dust go to sleep
I'm rocking my baby, and
babies don't keep.

■ Father, help me understand what few days I have to enjoy my little children. It won't be long before I will not be able to kiss them goodnight or drive them to school or help them decide what to wear. As their father and I are the primary influence in their lives for this brief span, help us use our time wisely. Don't let us squander our days on selfish pursuits or outside responsibilities only to live with regrets later. They will be children such a little while; help us make their childhood sparkle with bright memories.

He Grants Sleep

"*In vain you rise early and stay up late, toiling for food to eat—for he grants sleep to those he loves.*

Psalm 127:2

My sister-in-law wrote: "It's been a wild week here. Graham kicked the weekend off to an auspicious start by throwing up in the check-out lane at Pick 'n Save. I must have gone into shock, for I remember very little about the trip home.

"Lately, I have been doing a wonderful imitation of an absent-minded professor—without detailed lists I forget *everything*! It seems that once I bundle everyone into snowsuits, hats, mittens, boots, etc., I suddenly forget where it was we were going and why we were going there!"

I can identify. I think I have misplaced my mind. I used to think I was going crazy, but lately I've taken comfort in the fact that I'm still sane enough to recognize insanity when it hits me! I not only have come to recognize the symptoms, I have even determined a major cause for the bouts with temporary amnesia that are common among young mothers—extreme sleep deprivation.

Sleep deprivation seems to be a hazard of the trade. Mothers with infants or sick children are especially susceptible to this malady. For these mothers an uninterrupted night's sleep is only a daydream. And after one or two nights of insufficient sleep there is generally a noticeable decline in concentration level.

But sleepless nights are only half the problem. Suppose your child catches the latest virus. Your first priority is to care for your child, and everything else is set aside until later. That means you are left to play catch-up after your child recovers. You stay up later, rise earlier, and, if you're like me, become increasingly incoherent. Visine and caffeine become your traveling companions.

Walking with God works better! God places a high priority on rest and sleep. We require both, but often our priorities lie elsewhere. We will go to the trouble and expense to find a sitter to go shopping, to go to work, or to go out to eat . . . but to go to bed?

Often, even after periods where losing sleep is unavoidable, we relentlessly push ourselves, allowing little time to rest or recover. But sometimes the most spiritual thing we can do is sleep! Even if the housework doesn't get done immediately, even if we have to skip a church function or a meeting, even if we must cross an activity off our social calendar, we must carefully guard our energy reserves. Taking a nap isn't sinful! God sanctions sleep.

■ Lord, many of the things that occupy my thoughts and schedule really aren't worth losing sleep over. I confess that sometimes I feel as if everything depends on me, and getting work done is the top priority. Show me a healthy balance between activity and inactivity, working hard and resting well. Thank you for creating both day and night, allowing ample time for sleep.

One Thing I Do

"*But one thing I do: Forgetting what is behind and straining toward what is ahead, I press on toward the goal to win the prize for which God has called me heavenward in Christ Jesus.*

Philippians 3:13-14

My husband, frustrated by the constant pressure to spread himself too thin, said with exasperation, "My life is aimed like buckshot at the world!"

Have you, too, found it easy to shoot your energies "shotgun style," leaving a scattered pattern of tiny marks on your world, but no major indication of your efforts? On the other hand, do you find singleness of purpose hard to maintain?

If so, you need to collect your energy and direct it more accurately. First define what you're aiming at. Then at least you will know whether you hit it! We all need a goal or purpose in life.

We need to become "one thing" people: "one thing I do" said Paul (v. 13); "one thing I ask of the Lord" wrote the psalmist (Ps. 27:4); "one thing is needed" Jesus explained to Martha (Luke 10:42).

This "one thing" directed all of the apostle Paul's activities. His aim was to live out God's calling for his life for one reason: to glorify God.

We each need to determine God's calling in our lives, then set up goals accordingly. Through prayer and reading God's Word we will come to know God's will for us. Priorities can then fall into place—we are called to love and serve God, our spouse and family, our church, our community, etc. The *manner* in which we love and serve will be determined by our individual calling and gifts.

A purposeful life is worth the effort and self-discipline goals require. Maybe you're tired of going around in circles, but you're having a little trouble stopping the merry-go-round long enough to get off! Some days outside forces may temporarily manage to thwart every goal you set out to achieve. Don't be discouraged—God is merciful. We are given another chance.

Goals in themselves are no guarantee of success; we're to trust in God, not goals! But they are helpful in bringing order to our lives and directing us in satisfying and successful achievements. Outlook affects outcome. Even if not every goal is reached, the person who tries to do something and fails is still better off than the person who tries to do nothing and succeeds!

Target your life to seek out God's way. Forget about yesterday's failures and mistakes. They are forgiven. Put the past behind you and with the gentle leading of the Spirit, press on toward the goal. You may not always hit the mark, but let it be said that you gave it your best shot!

■ Lord, you know I'm guilty of pursuing too many things at once, and as a result, I fail to accomplish what you have called me to do. I ask for wisdom in determining your call, for self-discipline and perseverance in carrying it out.

God's Direction

"*This is what the Lord says . . . 'I am the Lord your God, who teaches you what is best for you, who directs you in the way you should go. If only you had paid attention to my commands, your peace would have been like a river, your righteousness like the waves of the sea.'*

Isaiah 48:17-18

A Chinese proverb says:

If we don't change our direction, we're likely to end up where we're headed.

There are times when we all need to check the direction of our lives. It's easy to get sidetracked pursuing success, material possessions, career advancement, or something else we perceive will make us happy. We don't always know what's best for us, and we may inattentively join others moving toward the wrong life's goals like cattle crowding an electric fence.

But we don't have to waste our time and effort seeking fulfillment by wandering aimlessly along trial-and-error trails. We can live in touch with God, who teaches us what's best, and directs us in the way we should go. When God guides, we avoid empty pursuits and painful disappointments. Living by God's counsel, we will succeed and prosper in the things that matter most. We'll not only end up where we're headed, we'll be abundantly satisfied when we get there!

■ All-knowing God, thank you for your Holy Spirit, who leads and guides me in your paths of love. Help me pay attention to the Spirit's voice and your patient calling so I may experience the peace and joy you desire for me. Thank you for having my best interest at heart.

Modeling the Message

"Fix these words of mine in your hearts and minds. . . . Teach them to your children, talking about them when you sit at home and when you walk along the road, when you lie down and when you get up.

Deuteronomy 11:18-19

Children learn by example. It's important for us to live by the standards we try to teach our kids. But that's not always easy! Franklin P. Jones was right when he commented, "Children are unpredictable. You never know what inconsistency they're going to catch you in next!"

Even in our areas of strength, we can expect to suffer momentary lapses from sainthood, as Terry can testify. Terry is the mother of three preschoolers. She sets a wonderful example for her children, particularly in respect to consistently maintaining a loving and gentle tone of voice. Terry doesn't raise her voice (truthfully!), and she won't allow her kids to do so—not even to call her from another room. Instead, she gently insists, "If you wish to speak to me, come to where I am."

One day, as Terry was upstairs making beds, and the little ones were downstairs playing, she heard her daughter shout, "Mom! Mom! M-o-m!"

Slightly annoyed, Terry walked to the stair rail and said, "Whitney, please come here."

No response. Then the calls resumed, "Mom! Mom!"

"Whitney, come here!" Terry called a little louder.

"Mom, come here!" Whitney echoed louder still.

And then our model mother became angry. "Whitney, you come here! Right now!" she yelled as loud as she could. As Whitney came to the bottom of the stairs, Terry continued in a crisp, staccato voice, "If you wish to speak to me, you come to where I am! How many times . . . ?" After her lecture, when she had finally calmed down a little, she asked, "Now *what* was so important that you needed to yell up here to get me?"

"Somebody's here," came the meek response from the bottom of the stairs.

Terry went down to face a room full of visitors—all of whom had heard clearly what had transpired. She said it was so traumatic, she can't remember to this day who was there! Thankfully, most of us will never have to face up to our moments of failure in similiar circumstances. But we do have to face up to the fact that we are not perfect. Relieving the stress of unrealistic expectations and allowing ourselves room to laugh at our mistakes will help keep parenting in perspective.

There's nothing wrong with modeling mistakes, as long as we also model the right response to them. The most helpful example for a child is seeing an imperfect parent sincerely trying to do God's will.

■ Father, I pray for my children whom you desire to love and serve you. They are yours, and you have given them to me to cherish and instruct. You want me to lead them to you. Please perfect me to the image of your Son so that I may accomplish your will.

"Man Looks at the Outward Appearance"

"*'The Lord does not look at the things man looks at. Man looks at the outward appearance, but the Lord looks at the heart.'*

1 Samuel 16:7

Even with the first pregnancy, ballooning from a 112-pound weakling to a Goodyear blimp seemed so—well—obvious! Then, as pregnancy became a regular occurrence (three of the next four turned out to be "good years") I became increasingly self-conscious.

I hated prenatal doctor visits. Routine weigh-ins made me feel like one of our fat cattle waiting around to reach shipping weight. Not to mention that I found the sterile-smelling examination room nauseating—literally. The car was knee-deep in cracker crumbs by the time I was delivered to delivery.

When I managed to take my eyes off my changing shape, which was pretty hard to miss, I enjoyed the curious stir of the tiny new life inside. I was awed at the privilege of participating in the creation of a precious child. Watching my shirt waltz from side to side as the baby performed an underwater ballet was quite entertaining. But during my mood swings, I wondered how such a tiny baby could take up such a large amount of space.

Some women feel beautiful when they're expecting. I felt big. And I was big. Then little. In again, out again, in again, out again—my inner perception of myself couldn't stretch with my elastic waistline.

Rotating between a 21- and 51-inch equator made me aware that my world was spinning on the wrong axis. My inner attitudes were revolving around my outward

appearance. Real beauty, I'd learned in the Bible, develops on the inside and shines through. But could it really make it through all those layers? Initially I had my doubts.

Instead of my outward appearance reflecting my inner contentment, it was wrecking it. I needed to repeat the lesson four times in order to understand that I was beautiful in God's sight, whether in size 5 or 45.

■ Lord, it's good for me to want to look my best, but it's so easy for me to lose your perspective. I confess that my outward appearance often affects my attitude, making me feel smugly self-confident when I think I look good, or incompetent and insecure when I don't. Help me work on being beautiful from the inside out. Give me eyes to see myself and others as you do, looking at the heart rather than the outward appearance.

Call to Me and I Will Answer

"*This is what the Lord says, he who made the earth, the Lord who formed it and established it—the Lord is his name: 'Call to me and I will answer you and tell you great and unsearchable things you do not know.'*

Jeremiah 33:2-3

Soon after our pastor and his wife purchased a new station wagon at an auction, they thought it would be fun for the family to get a third seat to fit in the back. They contacted an auto-parts dealer who used a computer network to check locations across the nation. And they began praying with their three small children, asking God to provide one the color and cost they needed.

Several months passed and nothing turned up. Only one person in Dallas, of the many they called, had a seat that would fit their car—and it was the wrong color and price. "At that point, we'd kind of given up on it," the father explained. "We began tempering our prayers; explaining to the kids that although God always does what's best for us, we don't always get what we want, and so on. . . . You know—the kind of things you tell the kids when *you've* given up hope!

"But the kids kept praying. Over a year after our first prayer, we found a third seat, less than 60 miles from home, that matched perfectly. I'm convinced that we got the car seat because three little kids simply wouldn't quit praying!"

Persistence is one element of effective prayer. Childlike faith, or confidence in God's ability and willingness to answer, is another. But isn't there more to prayer than accomplishing specific results?

Dr. Calvin Miller, in his excellent book *The Table of*

Inwardness, gives threefold advice: "First we should feel complete freedom to ask a loving Father for the desires of our heart. Second, we must agree that what we want can be set aside to meet the demands of a higher will. Third, our ultimate motivation for prayer should not be that we want something from God but that we want God."

■ Teach me to pray, Lord. And teach me to listen and look for your answers. Draw me closer to you in intimate communion, that I might experience the abundant joy of your fellowship.

MARTHA, WORRIED AND UPSET

Worried and Upset about Many Things

"*As Jesus and his disciples were on their way, he came to a village where a woman named Martha opened her home to him. She had a sister called Mary, who sat at the Lord's feet listening to what he said. But Martha was distracted by all the preparations that had to be made. She came to him and asked, 'Lord, don't you care that my sister has left me to do the work by myself? Tell her to help me!'*

'Martha, Martha,' the Lord answered, 'you are worried and upset about many things, but only one thing is needed. Mary has chosen what is better, and it will not be taken away from her.'

Luke 10:38-42

Hanging up the phone and switching off the light, I headed briskly toward the living room, smacking my middle toe on the corner of the oak high chair our son had pulled away from the table. With my husband still at a meeting and the kids in bed, I lay crumpled on the kitchen floor, blubbering over what had to be a broken toe. What timing! "How am I ever going to get things ready by Friday?" I groaned as I crawled to the bathroom for aspirins and a hot bath.

Earlier in the week, when the planned hostess had unexpected company, I had agreed to invite several couples over to get to know the young missionary family visiting our church. Of course I had no way of knowing then that the first-of-the-year scrimmage would leave a shortage of high school sitters. And I hadn't planned to be lying here in the tub—watching my toe swell to twice its normal size.

Friday noon arrived and I was starting to get past mildly concerned to all-out worried. Thanks to the help of a college friend, most of the cleaning was done. But the desserts weren't made, and we still had no sitter. On the bright side, I could limp on my toe, which wasn't broken after all, only sprained. I figured I could scrub and wax the kitchen floor while the kids were napping, and then bake a couple of bundt cakes.

By the time I finished removing the spots of playdough, and prying last week's Cheerios off the floor, the girls were awake and eager to "help." We managed to get the first cake in the oven with only minor fallout on the floor. (Why was it I thought the floor had to be waxed *before* I made and served crumbly cake?)

Half way through the second cake I noticed the full carton of eggs—still on the counter. All those hands at work, and not one of us added the eggs? I glanced in the oven for confirmation: one very flat chocolate cake. "What could be worse?" I muttered. "What will they think of someone who supposedly feeds a family of six and can't make a cake from a box mix?"

"I'm not going to get upset," I told myself with agitation. "I'll serve the other cake first and pray for small appetites." After frosting the cakes, I retreated upstairs to change clothes.

Back in the kitchen, I caught our two-year-old eating icing off the cake (the one *with* eggs), stuffing it into his mouth by the fistful! Crumbs scattered across the counter and floor like speckles on a bird's egg as I spanked his hand.

"No! No!" I exploded. (So much for not being upset.) Luckily most of the cake was untouched. Setting it safely out of reach, I planned to slice it later.

I had just finished cleaning up the mess when the first guests arrived. Greeting them with a forced smile, I settled them in the living room. Then, sending the older girls to play upstairs, I dashed back into the kitchen intending to apologize to our

toddler before slicing the cake.

Ouch! There he was again, on top of the counter bent over the cake, biting off a second helping.

Even though our guests weren't the least bit bothered by the crumpled confections, and the spiritual impact of the evening didn't seem affected, my attitude was less appealing than the cakes. Maybe there's a *little* "Martha" in me after all!

■ Father, when I have company coming I turn all "Martha." I become worried and upset over so many things. Help me to focus on the people, not preparations. Forgive the pride in me that wants everything to be perfect, and the insecurity in me that worries about what others might think if it isn't. Thank you for being more patient with your child than I am with mine.

A Cheerful Giver

“*Each man should give what he has decided in his heart to give, not reluctantly or under compulsion, for God loves a cheerful giver.*

2 Corinthians 9:7

Did you hear about the simplified tax form suggested by Stanton Delaplane? It read: How much money did you make last year? Mail it in.

For many people, paying taxes is a prime example of reluctant giving. Unlike Uncle Sam, God allows us complete freedom to choose the amount we give to the Lord. God wants us to make sure that our hearts are in our gifts, that we give from right motives, not under compulsion. God makes us stewards of what is God's, trusting us to give generously. God prompts our hearts to give, not reluctantly, but cheerfully.

Offerings that are given freely and wholeheartedly please our Lord. The simplified giving guideline suggested by God might read: How much money did you make last year? Give gladly.

■ Merciful Father, thank you for your generosity toward me. Thank you for the freedom to give willingly and according to my ability. Help me to give unselfishly and cheerfully.

Apart from Me You Can Do Nothing

"I am the vine; you are the branches. If a man remains in me and I in him, he will bear much fruit; apart from me you can do nothing.'

John 15:5

Returning from a shopping trip, my four preschoolers and I were wheeling down a nearly deserted county highway. Packed into our aging silver import with groceries and all, like sardines in a tin can, we were beginning to pick up our own peculiar odor. Something indeed smelled fishy! With no feed lots in sight, I knew someone must have chosen this particular moment to do his daily duty.

Fortunately, we were nearly home, and I reached for the vent. Unfortunately, my daughter chose that exact moment to shove a large, pink balloon in my face. "Look Mommy, I can blow up a balloon!"

I jerked upright, struggling to get some glimpse of the road. "No, not now! I can't look now, I'm driving!"

Startled by my outbreak, she released the balloon, and it began buzzing around in front of my face like a mosquito. Distracted by the aerobatics, I failed to notice that our two-year-old had slipped out of his seat belt and weasled between the front bucket seats to check out all the fun.

"I sit on Mommy's lap," he announced as he let go of the seat to fall backward across my arms.

Luckily (or maybe not), one hand maintained its grip on the steering wheel, causing us to lurch into the left lane. Not being fond of accordian doors, I thought it would be best to return to our side of the road in the near future, particularly since an oncoming car was only a half mile off.

I righted our course, simultaneously shoving my son to the passenger side. He landed upright in his sister's lap, but not before he snatched the keys. Wondering what the drivers behind us were thinking, I intercepted his hand and shoved in the clutch. Jabbing the key back in the ignition, I was dismayed to find that we continued to coast while the engine idled. Everything wasn't suddenly all right again. I pumped the gas wildly.

Slowing to an embarrassing 14 mph, I finally realized that my little troublemaker had also kicked the gear shift into neutral as he had made his flying exit.

With no place to pull over, I settled for severely scolding the kids, lecturing on "what might have beens" for the remainder of the drive. After my heart had slowed down and we were turning into our drive, I looked at the episode with more objectivity.

Any untrained observer could have pointed out that, (1) cars don't run when you turn off the power, and (2) no matter how much power the engine has, you still have to put the transmission in gear.

Sort of like my Christian walk, I mused. Trying to make up ground in the Christian journey apart from the power of God, is like expecting the car to run with the engine turned off. The verse "Apart from me, you can do nothing" came to mind. But, I continued the analogy, there would be no "*you* can do" unless the "you" got in gear and did something. Both dependency and industry are needed to keep things running smoothly and avoid mishaps.

■ Lord, when I'm getting nowhere in my Christian life, help me remember this verse. Sometimes I try everything *I* can think of to get where *I* want to go, forgetting that apart from you I can do nothing. But, other times when I seek your direction and power, looking closely to make sure I'm keeping the switch active, I still wonder why things aren't getting accomplished. Maybe I'm idling around in neutral. Help me get in gear when I need to, finding a proper balance between dependency and industry.

Let Your Light Shine

"'Let your light shine before men, that they may see your good deeds and praise your Father in heaven.'

Matthew 5:16

"This little light of mine, I'm gonna let it shine. . ." the kids sang exuberantly, repeating the familiar chorus over and over as they danced around the living room.

As I watched I found myself thinking of my own "little light." Have you ever questioned your witness? Is it shining strongly or has it been flickering so much lately it probably looks more like an S.O.S. message in Morse Code than a beacon for Jesus?

Many lights are fading fast. Some are burning out entirely. Often it is because we have given up the notion that God is the only true source of light, and are trying to uphold our "good-guy image" in the church and community by doing good deeds using our own power.

We get over-impressed with ourselves and pick up the idea that the brightest light is the one whose witness shines farthest. We like flashy ministries, the bigger the better! But as Dr. Oswald Smith used to say, the light that shines the farthest will shine the brightest at home. As a missionary once put it, there is no use taking a lamp to Indonesia that will not burn at home.

How does God intend for us to shine? "Those who are wise will shine like the brightness of the heavens, and those who lead many to righteousness, like the stars for ever and ever" (Dan. 12:3). Wisdom and witness are the key determinants for radiant living.

As we live wisely, the world will be attracted by our light, and we will have ample opportunity to witness. Then the glow of our active faith will indeed bring glory to God.

■ Father, I want to live in the light of your Word. I ask for wisdom. I want your love and hope to shine through me to those who live in darkness. Don't let the shadow of sin in my life destroy my witness, but let your light shine in my heart.

In the Same Way

“‘Do not judge, or you too will be judged. For in the same way you judge others, you will be judged, and with the measure you use, it will be measured to you.’

Matthew 7:1

My family often laughs about things that happened when we kids were little—like the day my sister played “barber shop” with the neighbor girl and me. According to the story, my sister washed my hair in Vasoline and gave our playmate a haircut—chopping off her long blonde hair in uneven jags, nearly to the scalp in places! To my mother’s dismay, even a quick trip to the beautician did little to conceal the damage.

As I grew older and heard this story retold at family gatherings, I began to wonder, Where was Mom when this episode was taking place? How could things have gotten so far out of hand while she was there to check on us? I guess that was my naive version of “What kind of a mother would . . . ?”

Then I got married and had children of my own!

One summer afternoon, when the girls were two and three, I laid them down for naps and came downstairs just as the phone rang. The friend calling wanted to know if it was a good time to stop by for a visit. We chatted a while, and I encouraged her to come. When I hung up the phone, I could hear the girls giggling, so I went up to check on them.

As I climbed the stairs, I could tell the laughter was coming from our bedroom, not theirs, and I suspected mischief. Even so, I was not prepared for the sight that greeted me as I stepped in the doorway.

Erin and Martha had stripped off all of their clothes and all of the sheets on our waterbed. Then they had emptied an economy-sized bottle of baby oil on the vinyl mattress. They were now dripping wet with oil, gleefully sliding across the slick surface like playful sea otters on ice!

Martha noticed me first. "Look, Mommy!" she squealed with delight, as she dove off the headboard and slid across the king-sized mattress, spraying droplets of oil in every direction. Erin was close behind. Her slippery, little body spurted up and over Martha before sprawling against the wall at the edge of the bed, ending up beside her sister in a pile of giggles. Other oil splotches on the wall, and the soggy sheets on the floor marked earlier crash-landing sites.

I left the room to regain my composure and get the camera. When I returned, I documented the scene for future generations before handling the discipline.

Just as I was carrying the girls downstairs for baths, my friend arrived. As I plopped my messy moppets into the warm water and added degreaser, I briefly explained what had happened. My friend's eyes widened in disbelief, and she burst out laughing. Although she was too kind to say, I knew she was thinking, And where were you while all this was happening? How could things have gotten so far out of hand?

■ Lord, thank you for the humorous things that happen to keep us humble! Remind me of my own slip-ups when I am tempted to be critical of others. Help me to treat others kindly, with the same understanding I hope to receive.

Aim for Perfection?

"*Aim for perfection, listen to my appeal, be of one mind, live in peace. And the God of love and peace will be with you.*

2 Corinthians 13:11

"Our kids are perfect examples—of normal children!" my husband once commented. He wasn't implying that we had a faultless family, but quite the opposite—that normal children come equipped with imperfections.

So do normal Christians. The Bible tells us that everyone sins and falls short of God's standards. Nobody's perfect. But even so, we can be perfectly pleasing to God.

Hannah Whitall Smith, author of the classic *The Christian's Secret of a Happy Life,* explained it this way: "The little babe may be all that a babe could be, or ought to be, and may therefore perfectly please its mother; and yet it is very far from being what that mother would wish it to be when the years of maturity shall come.

"The apple in June is a perfect apple for June; but it is very different from the apple in October, which is a perfected apple.

"God's works are perfect in every stage of their growth. Man's works are never perfect until they are in every respect complete."

She went on to explain that Christian perfection is the process of growing in grace, and conforming, day by day and hour by hour, to the image of Christ. This maturity cannot be reached in a moment. But the sanctification the Scriptures urge does not consist in maturity of growth, but in purity of heart, and this may be as complete today as tomorrow.

By faith, we are to aim at perfection, trusting in the work of God's Holy Spirit to cause growth. And while we do, we are perfectly pleasing to God!

■ Gracious Father, thank you for loving and accepting me just as I am—less than perfect. Thank you for delighting in me, for I know you take delight in those who put their hope in your unfailing love. And I praise you God; your lovingkindness toward me is everlasting!

Crave Spiritual Milk

"*Like newborn babies, crave pure spiritual milk, so that by it you may grow up in your salvation, now that you have tasted that the Lord is good.*

1 Peter 2:2

Three of our four children could not digest milk at birth. Breast milk, cow's milk, fake milk—you name it, we tried it! And it didn't work. So we nursed them on Pregestimil, a "predigested" baby formula. In this formula, the long-chain proteins and carbohydrates normally found in milk have been broken down chemically for easier digestion.

Even while they were being fed intravenously, each newborn craved milk. Having to begin with only two-ounce feedings of quarter-strength Pregestimil, every three hours around the clock, did little to appease their hunger! Once they had tasted a little, they longed for more.

When it comes to spiritual growth, we are told to crave the pure milk of the Word like newborn babies—that's a pretty strong desire! Elsewhere, the Bible calls the Word of God spiritual food, meat, and the bread of life.

These portions from God's Word can help you taste and see that the Lord is good. But if these short passages are all you are reading, you are not exactly enjoying a banquet! These "two-ounce" servings may give you a taste of the Word of God, but they can hardly do more than whet your appetite. Just as snacking will not result in a nutritional diet, these readings alone will not satisfy your spiritual hunger for God.

These meals are like "predigested" formula. Spiritual food has been prepared for you by breaking down longer passages of Scripture into bite-sized pieces that can be more easily digested during a busy day. There's nothing wrong with occasional "fast-food," but God has prepared a feast of rich food for us to enjoy. How much better it is to dine in person with the Lord!

■ Father, I have "tasted that the Lord is good." I know you want to be personal in my life. I realize your thoughts don't have to come to me secondhand, for you desire to speak directly to me from your Word. Thank you for the many others whose nourishing ideas have helped me grow, but teach me to come first to you to be fed. Remind me to put everyone else's book down when it's time to come to dinner!

A Voice?

"Whether you turn to the right or to the left, your ears will hear a voice behind you, saying, 'This is the way; walk in it.'

Isaiah 30:21

Sometimes it strikes me that Mary and Martha had it easy when they listened to Jesus. They knew with certainty it was Jesus talking, and they understood what it was he said—none of this "still, small voice" stuff!

These sisters never had to wonder: Does Jesus still speak to his followers today? Is it always through this voice from within? What if I don't hear anything when I listen? What if I do—how can I be sure it is really God who is talking?

A few years ago I came across a list of guidelines written by Dr. James Dobson based on a booklet by Martin Wells Knapp that helped me immensely in learning to distinguish the voice of God from other unreliable inner impulses. Since some impressions are not valid, it is not safe to assume that a feeling or thought is sent from God. Sometimes the "voice" may be from God, from Satan, or of our own making. Therefore Dr. Dobson's criteria for testing every impression and leading are essential for everyone who wants to listen at the feet of Jesus.

Here is Dr. Dobson's list, taken from his book *Emotions, Can You Trust Them?* (Regal Books, 1980).

- *Is it scriptural?* This test involves taking more than a random proof text. It means studying what the whole Bible teaches. Use a concordance, search the Scriptures as did the Bereans (see Acts 17:11). Evaluate tentative leanings against the immutable Word of God.

- *Is it right?* Every expression of God's will can be expected to conform to God's universal principles of morality and decency. If an impression would result in the depreciation of human worth or the integrity of the family or related traditional Christian values, it must be viewed with suspicion.
- *Is it providential?* The third test requires every impression to be considered in the light of providential circumstances, such as: are the necessary doors opening or closing? Do circumstances permit the implementation of what I feel to be God's will? Is the Lord speaking to me through events?
- *Is it reasonable?* The final criterion against which the will of God is measured relates to the appropriateness of the act. Does it make sense? Is it consistent with the character of God to require it? Will this act contribute to the kingdom?

By using these guidelines, we can hear the voice of Jesus speaking personally to us, even as Mary and Martha did. God sent the Holy Spirit to assure us of this guidance. As the Bible teaches, we can hear God's voice saying, "This is the way; walk in it" (Isa. 30:21).

■ Father, thank you for your desire to lead and guide us personally in our choices. Help me discover the "still, small voice" of the Holy Spirit within me. Give me the discernment to recognize your voice in the midst of the other influences seeking to exercise power over my thoughts. I come confidently to sit at your feet, anticipating two-way conversation in prayer. And I will listen as you speak in many other ways each day, especially through your Word.

Let the Little Children Come

"*People were bringing little children to Jesus to have him touch them, but the disciples rebuked them. When Jesus saw this, he was indignant. He said to them, 'Let the little children come to me, and do not hinder them, for the kingdom of God belongs to such as these.'*

Mark 10:13-15

Standing over one very alert two-year-old (who was supposed to be napping), I switched to plan B. So much for an uninterrupted quiet time today.

"Well, Lord, how am I going to do this?" I sighed in exasperation and paused for his response.

Startled by a sudden quiet (an immediate indication that all is not well), I surveyed the room in search of my sleepless son. I should have known better than to pray with my eyes closed!

I quickly spotted him. In the blinking of an eye he'd hopped off the bed, flown across the room, and landed in my jewelry box. Now my little love bird was contentedly pulling the backs off my pierced earrings. I resisted my initial reaction to save my newest set of pop beads—which would occasion an outburst—knowing he could quietly entertain himself while I read.

Picking up my Bible, I opened it to Joshua and began to read where I'd left off. Joshua and his army were just getting ready to circle the city of Jericho. One lap into the incident I noticed that I, too, was hearing footsteps.

"What are you reading, Mommy?" my four-year-old queried.

"A story about a marching band," I responded, waiting for her to plop in my lap and beg me to keep reading. I briefly explained who Joshua was, then began again with history's first round trip.

More footsteps. Another preschooler appeared in the doorway. At this rate it was going to take Joshua more than seven days to get the job done.

"We're reading about Joshua and the battle of Jericho," the younger explained. "He had the first marching band."

"I know already," her sister replied. "Last summer Dad taught me the song they played."

My eyes widened as she began an animated demonstration, marching around the room singing loudly, "Joshua fit the battle of Jericho, Jericho. . . ."

Daughter number two and son number one followed her out the bedroom and joined the procession. Recognizing that things were quickly getting out of hand, I stepped in like the Pied Piper, heading for a larger room. Collapsing to the floor on "when the walls came tumbling down," I tried to get back to the written version. "Songs are a great way to learn and think about things that happened in the Bible, but Joshua. . . ."

A sharp squeal from the next room informed me that all our commotion had wakened the baby. What luck. Now they were four-strong. I thought back to my prechild days: "Lord, remember when I used to take long walks, letting nature draw me closer to you in praise and worship?"

As the kids dashed over to the crib, disrupting my thoughts, I was struck by a rather profound observation: Children, too, can walk, and babies come in a portable model!

"Get in the wagon, we're going for a walk," I announced rather abruptly, sounding like a quarterback at the snap. The kids looked delighted and raced out the door, earning at least one clipping penalty before reaching the yard line.

Leaning over the crib to meet tiny, upstretched arms,

I consoled myself with the thought that I might catch a little time alone to talk with God later, after their dad came home, or they'd gone to bed. But more disconcerting thoughts followed. Why was I unwilling to relinquish my right to private time with God? Was I resenting the intrusion into our fellowship or any change in it? Was I insisting we spend time alone, while Jesus was whispering, "Let the little children come . . ."?

■ Jesus, sometimes I resent having the kids interrupt everything I try to do—even my quiet time alone with you. Forgive me for only wanting what's easiest for me. Please give me your love, your open arms to gather our little ones into my lap and share with them the joy of knowing their heavenly Father. Help me make use of the opportunities you give through stories, songs, and nature to teach them about you. And Lord, you know I need you, and I need time alone with you; please work it out.

Be Patient

“*Be completely humble and gentle; be patient, bearing with one another in love.*

Ephesians 4:2

The trouble with being patient is that it cannot be done unless there is a circumstance which would make us impatient! Which means that we must do precisely the thing we do not wish to do, and do not do well—*wait*.

Wait—for the preschooler to put on his or her shoes and socks, for God to answer our deepest prayers, for the proper time to develop our talents. And, as if it's not enough to have to wait, we're expected to do it calmly without becoming irritated or provoked! That's patience.

That's impossible! It's a good thing the Bible tells us that Jesus has unlimited patience for us to draw on, because the circumstances surrounding motherhood give ample opportunity to prove that our own supply is insufficient. I even find myself praying much like the joke expresses, "Lord give me patience—*right now*!" But God does everything in his time.

■ Lord, given the opportunities I've had to practice being patient, I've not made much progress. Sometimes it seems that everyone is doing all they can to try my patience—and it's working! Father, I can't do it on my own. I ask you to fill me with your patience, especially toward my family, for this would honor you. And Lord, let me respond patiently toward you, knowing that you will do just what you say in your time.

"Because Men Do Not Believe"

"*'When he [the Holy Spirit] comes, he will convict the world of guilt in regard to sin and righteousness and judgment: in regard to sin, because men do not believe in me.'*

John 16:8-9

Did you hear about the young mother whose little boy complained that his head was hurting? When she took him to see the doctor, the doctor asked, "Does your son get headaches often?"

"No, but he's a carrier!" the mother replied.

Have you found there are certain headaches involved in raising small children? The noise, the mess, and the interruptions are but a few examples. Everyone encounters difficulties in doing anything worthwhile, and parenting is no exception.

Still, in discouraging moments it's easy to end up wondering whether you are really cut out to be a parent. You may even find yourself thinking, "Did God really plan this, or am I the victim of my own stupidity? I just can't deal with kids!" When such thoughts cross our minds, we aren't doubting ourselves so much as questioning God.

The sin that encompasses all other sins is unbelief. By rejecting the idea that God can handle our problems or equip us to handle them, we are saying we don't believe God has our best interests in mind. We don't acknowledge God's superior judgment that children are a blessing, not a trial!

Jesus said the Holy Spirit would convict us of guilt in regard to sin. Specifically, "in regard to sin, because men do not believe in me" (John 16:9). Not believing that God is bigger than our petty problems is sin. We need to cut out all the excuses, confess our lack of trust and receive forgiveness with thanksgiving.

We can trust God for wisdom, for the strength to change, and for the ability to handle our difficult moments. We can take our "headaches" to the Great Physician! He alone knows how to remedy the situation.

■ Lord, please change me or my circumstances—we're not getting along so well together these days! I want to believe you are able to cause all things to work together for good, but I confess that I sometimes doubt your ability to handle my problems. Forgive me. Help me in my unbelief.

Making the Most

"*Be very careful, then, how you live—not as unwise but as wise, making the most of every opportunity, because the days are evil.*

Ephesians 5:15-16

Guess which hand?" Cindy asked.

"That one!" Erin pointed as she eagerly stretched out her hand to take the new book. Getting a new book from Cindy, her nurse, was always a highlight of my daughter's hospital stays. Leaning forward, I caught a glimpse of the title, *Alexander and the Terrible, Horrible, No Good, Very Bad Day*.

The book was appropriate. Looking back on how her day had gone, I knew Erin could identify with Alexander. It had been a difficult morning.

Earlier that day, Erin's doctor had told her, "We made a little mistake at the close of your angiogram. We're really sorry that you're going to end up with some swelling and a pretty big bruise from the internal bleeding. It doesn't happen very often, and we sure feel bad that it happened to you." He went on to explain she would need to stay overnight in intensive care, stay home from school the rest of the week, and stay quiet through the weekend. She had been expecting a routine out-patient procedure.

Erin took the news well. She knew it meant she would have to miss the Mother's Day brunch her kindergarten class had been looking forward to on Thursday. Participating in the long jump at the end-of-the-year track meet was also ruled out. I knew she was disappointed and hurting.

I was glad Erin could at least enjoy the book. She certainly didn't enjoy the "yucky tasting" medicine!

I climbed in bed beside her and began reading. Erin snuggled closer as I turned the pages, then announced, "It's supposed to be Daddy's turn, isn't it?" Glad for the chance to get up and stretch, I turned the book over to my husband and wandered toward the window.

As I gazed through the window at the bright spring morning, memories of our recent trip to the zoo came to my mind. Just two days earlier, on a day just as beautiful, our family had gone with friends to the zoo to celebrate Mother's Day. Good friends, good times, good weather—now that was a good day! Gratitude for the love and family closeness we had shared welled up inside me. "Thank you so much, Lord, for such a special opportunity to spend time together."

I turned from the window and returned to the chair at Erin's bedside. She was feeling sleepy after the story and was ready to take a much-needed nap. Between the bright lights and the computers clicking, monitors buzzing, people talking, and television competing to be heard, it was nearly impossible for her to rest. Just as she finally dozed off, the nurse arrived to take "vitals" which, in my opinion, were not vital. Even a healthy child would feel lousy after two days in this environment, I thought in frustration.

Eventually Erin drifted off to sleep. After her nap we spent the rest of the afternoon watching videos, drinking Pepsi, and drawing pictures together.

"I want to read my new book again, Mommy," Erin asked at the close of the day. So we read our way through Alexander's no good, very bad day one more time.

Hoping to give Erin a chance to share her feelings, when I finished reading I asked, "Did you have a good day or a bad day?"

"A good day," she replied, "We got to watch four videos and read books. . . ."

Her voice trailed off as she looked down at the picture she had drawn. Instinctively my eyes followed hers. In her picture a little blonde girl was holding bright balloons under a smiling sun. Across the top she had printed, "I love you Mommy."

I read the words slowly, blinking back the tears. "I love you too, Erin," I whispered. "I'm glad you had a good day."

■ O Lord, sometimes the needs of my children are so strikingly simple . . . they need *me*. It's humbling to think of the value they place on time spent with me.

I confess that I'm often too preoccupied with making dinner or making money to be occupied with them. I haven't made the most of every opportunity to be with them; to love them in the way they perceive love. Help me live more carefully and wisely. Lord, let me be there for them. Let their childhood be full of good days we shared together.

MARY, AT THE LORD'S FEET

Mary, at the Lord's Feet

“*Martha opened her home to him [Jesus]. She had a sister called Mary, who sat at the Lord's feet listening to what he said.*

Luke 10:38-39

Is true religion lived in private or in public? The comfortable answer is in private. The biblical answer is both places.

Three times in the New Testament we find Mary at the feet of Jesus in the presence of others. Once to listen, once for comfort at the death of her brother (John 11:32), and once for a service of love (John 12:3).

Few among us are as bold as Mary was in approaching Jesus, especially in public. Her humble confidence rested in her knowledge of his love, their private bond. She knew he would understand why she had come, even if others misunderstood. She trusted in his friendship.

The presence of others was not the issue; the presence of Christ was. Mary didn't intend to make a public display of her religion. She wasn't trying to impress anyone or inspire them to do what she did. She acted out of love. She was never too self-conscious to express her concern for Christ in front of people.

In public and in private, Mary lived a life of consistent devotion.

■ Lord Jesus, help me to live consistently close to you, whether or not others are present. Give me your boldness when the need of the moment requires it. Help me not to worry about the public response to my faith, and instead concern myself with sitting at your feet!

Greet One Another with a Kiss!

"*Greet one another with a kiss of love.*

1 Peter 5:14

A lonely man commented, "I'll get married when I find a woman who greets me at the door the way my dogs do."

An interesting comment! Our greetings reveal the value we place on people. How do you and your spouse greet each other at the end of the work day? How do you greet your kids?

A familiar routine tends to disguise the significance of greetings. We may begin to take each other for granted, hardly acknowledging the arrival of those we love. Or we may become so enamored with the busy-ness of our day that we don't take the time to stop what we're doing and welcome others, unless, of course, they're strangers.

Greeting someone properly builds their self-esteem. It communicates that they are important; that you appreciate them enough to acknowledge their arrival. Something as simple as eye contact, affirming touch, and an encouraging word of greeting can communicate "I love you," and "I've missed you," and "I'm glad you're home!"

So greet your family with a kiss of love. Begin today!

■ Father, remind me to greet my husband and children with transparent eagerness and love. I want them to know that our home is the place they are always welcome, wanted, and loved.

Sing and Make Music!

"Speak to one another with psalms, hymns and spiritual songs. Sing and make music in your heart to the Lord.

Ephesians 5:19

Have you ever been lost in activity, when suddenly you catch a song on the radio or a snatch of melody someone is humming that triggers a flood of memories? For me it is common.

I hear a man whistling one of Dad's songs and I am again a child with my fishing pole and a basket of worms. Or maybe I am bouncing along a sandhill road singing merrily with my brother, my sister, and Dad. I still laugh at the many times we would start on a familiar melody only to mess up completely within three measures when Dad entered with a harmony or round!

So many of my childhood memories are wrapped up in music. A simple chorus can open up past scenes of three preschoolers crowding in for their turn to "play" the accordian in Dad's arms, or the same three little squirts fighting over who would get to sit on the piano bench beside him! I can't hear Dean Martin or Bing Crosby without hearing Dad sing along in a rich, bass voice. Christmas carols always remind me of the time he spent coaching us for church programs.

My dad died when I was 12, but the richness of his legacy lives on. His love of music and my early experiences with music have wonderfully enriched my adult life. Music continues to provide hours of enjoyment in our home. (Even now, as I type, our toddler opens my guitar case and begins tugging at the strings. He looks up, asking hopefully, "Mommy! Play?") Our kids now sing away the miles in the backseat with familiar refrains. My dad's laughter echoes in my mind as they, too, mess up the melody when their father enters with the harmony or a round!

I wish every child could be given such a heritage! Music is one of God's most precious gifts. Music reaches our hearts with messages of love and truth, permanently etching into our memory such words as "Jesus loves me, this I know." It isn't surprising that God repeatedly commands us to sing!

Sing with your children. Whether your voice is concert quality or plain, old garden variety will not matter to them. Laughter, love, and spiritual truth can all be communicated through songs—even if they are sung rather poorly! Listening together to concerts, church choirs, recitals, or recordings is also a wonderful way to bring music into your home life.

Memories of my father and his music fill our home, and through this music his legacy lives. What will your child remember? I remember music!

■ Lord, help me to begin my own living legacy of music. Let our family sing your word, and share your love through song. Teach us to "make melody in our hearts" to you, as we are filled with thanksgiving and praise.

One Handful of Rest

“ *One handful of rest is better than two fists full of labor and striving after wind.*

Ecclesiastes 4:6 NASB

A troubled friend confided, “I spend about an hour and a half getting ready, an hour and a half commuting, five hours in class or studying for my CPA exam, five or more hours at work, an hour and a half working out, an hour or so eating, and around an hour in Bible study and prayer each day. We like to go out a lot on weekends. And I'm assistant Sunday school superintendent so I have to get to church a little early. We host the couples study on Sunday evening, so I spend a little time straightening up in the afternoon. Do you think I'm under stress, or is it just that time of month?”

“You've heard of burning the candle at both ends? Well, you're putting wicks where there aren't any!” I responded.

“I just don't want to get lazy or lay around all day,” she explained.

“There's quite a difference between being idle and being suicidal!” I teased. “Do you think you could find some middle ground?”

There's a lot of middle ground available these days. Many people have vacated the position. Often they don't realize that time is like money; we do not live on an inexhaustible supply. If we spend a dollar here, we do not have it to spend elsewhere. The same is true of time and energy. Once spent, it is gone. But typically, we don't get scared until we almost run out!

Financial advisors say that if we live within our means by a wide enough margin, budgeting is unnecessary. In the same way, a daily schedule budgeting every available moment of our day is unnecessary *if* we live well within the bounds of our emotional and physical resources. By allowing a cushion, perhaps an hour of "do nothing" time each day, we can accommodate the unexpected problems of our day without overdrawing our energy reserves.

My friend already saw the negative outcomes of continuing her life-style: digestion problems, decreased productivity, stress. She had really wanted to hear someone support her in her decision to quit working. Then she would be able to spend more time with her husband, catch up on her letter writing, study harder, call her sister more often, build more friendships, get back to her cross-stitch projects. . . .

■ Father, all of us can change our schedules, but changing our *mindset* is more difficult! It's so easy to pick up extra projects until people are pushed out of my life. I know that allowing myself to overdo it "just until I'm caught up" is striving after wind. Help me rest from my scurrying and worrying long enough to learn how to love and be loved.

A Father to the Fatherless

“*A father to the fatherless, a defender of widows, is God in his holy dwelling.*

Psalm 68:5

There are scattered moments in every person's life that dramatically change the rest of their life. When I was 12, I faced a moment of crisis. My father was killed in a car accident.

I was especially close to my dad, and I took his death very hard. In my loneliness, I searched for answers to painful questions: Why did God let the person I loved most die? Where was God when the accident occurred—why didn't God prevent it?

I looked in the Bible for answers. Starting with page one, as any young girl would, I read through to the back cover. One phrase stuck with me—God is "a father of the fatherless."

I remember feeling a keen awareness that I had to make a choice. I could turn from God, blaming him for my father's death; or I could turn to God, accepting his offer to love and comfort me. I prayed simply, "If you will be my Father, God, I will be your child."

Over the years, God has been faithful to his word, protecting me and providing for me at every turn. I've never regretted my decision to trust God.

My experience underscores the importance of those few profound moments in each person's life, where a significant choice is to be made. Moments when the choice to walk with God, or to go our own way, will have consequences for the rest of our lives. It is at such times that our compassionate Father draws closest, whispering love and hope in our hearts.

■ Father, when I am faced with difficult times and decisions, give me the faith to trust you and believe your Word. I pray for those who are lonely and hurting right now. Draw them into your family. Help them to turn to you and be comforted.

A WOMAN NAMED MARTHA

A Woman Named Martha

"*As Jesus and his disciples were on their way, he came to a village where a woman named Martha opened her home to him. She had a sister called Mary, who sat at the Lord's feet listening to what he said. But Martha was distracted by all the preparations that had to be made. She came to him and asked, 'Lord, don't you care that my sister has left me to do the work by myself? Tell her to help me!'*

'Martha, Martha,' the Lord answered, 'you are worried and upset about many things, but only one thing is needed. Mary has chosen what is better, and it will not be taken away from her.'

Luke 10:38-42

When you read this story, with whom do you tend to identify? It can be assumed that the correct response should be Mary, if you're a good Christian. But is that necessarily true? I think Martha has received a lot of bad press!

Each woman has her own blend of positive and negative characteristics. Martha opened her home to Jesus; she was hospitable. She served him. She was competent and organized. (She even planned what Mary should be doing!) She was willing to work hard. She came to Jesus with her problem. True, Martha made too much of a production out of the meal and as a result was worried and bothered by the details, but she did it from a desire to please.

Maybe being a "Martha" isn't all bad!

■ Father, teach me to imitate Martha in her willingness to work hard to serve you. Help me see the physical needs of others and move to meet them, as she did. Let me be willing to talk frankly to you about my grievances instead of griping to others.

Thank you that we all have strengths as well as weaknesses.

In Your Anger

“*'In your anger do not sin': Do not let the sun go down while you are still angry, and do not give the devil a foothold.*

Ephesians 4:26

A young man at a dinner party was discussing a recent squabble he'd had with his wife. He had come home late from work to find her fed up with the kids, with life in general, and with him in specific. "Have you ever stepped into a situation where someone thinks the whole world just went over the edge, and you're the part of the edge that crumbled?" he asked. "She said she needed room to herself—I figured she'd have more space to be alone if *I* left!"

Looking back on the situation, it sounded amusing—even his wife was laughing. But you could tell it had not been a laughing matter at the time!

God takes anger seriously, and so should we. The Bible says, "In your anger do not sin." We are to exercise self-control over our conduct and our words, even when we feel angry. (Notice that it does not say *if* you get angry! You will. But anger in itself is not sin. Improper response to anger is.)

Some things should never be said, no matter how hot the argument, no matter how angry we are. But often in the heat of the moment, we do not think clearly. Therefore, we must decide for ourselves *beforehand* just what things are really "out of bounds." We must resolve that we *never* resort to saying anything about those areas of vulnerability too painful to mention in an angry exchange.

In the same way, physical limits on our actions should be determined long before our tempers are riled and our adrenalin is pumping. Physical and emotional abuse, or any milder form of expressing anger in hurtful ways, is sin, because it is so contrary to love. And we are called to love one another as the Father loves us.

We are also told to keep short accounts, to settle quarrels within the day they occur whenever possible. If you are both too tired and upset to talk things over, you may want to agree to postpone the discussion until you're rested and cooled off. But be sure to keep the appointment.

Avoiding confrontation is not a long-term solution. Even though she did have more space when he left, they still had to share the same bathroom in the morning!

■ Father, evil seems to be winning out in the world, and it tries to win out in our home—a little at a time. With each outburst of anger, inconsiderate action, and unkind word, I am giving the devil a foothold from which to launch his attack on our family stronghold. It is not only the evil "out there" that threatens, it is the evil nature *in me* that seeks to destroy our home. Forgive me! Change me! Heal the damage I have done in my relationships. Lead me in your ways of love, O God.

We All Stumble

"*We all stumble in many ways. If anyone is never at fault in what he says, he is a perfect man, able to keep his whole body in check.*

James 3:2

My husband fumbled with the alarm clock, then bolted upright. "We're late!" he exclaimed. "You get Erin's clothes and I'll get breakfast. We might be able to get her to school on time if we hurry."

I jumped out of bed and rushed toward the stairs. Somewhere between the first step and the last, I slipped on the sock that matched the one I couldn't find a mate to the day before. Sliding face-first down the remaining stairs, I skidded into the kitchen, jamming my toe against the doorjamb in the process. (This time the bone broke!)

As I was lying there, face down with tears in my eyes, my husband came down the stairs. Stepping over me, he remarked, "Don't worry. The kids messed with the alarm again. We've got plenty of time."

At that point, a number of unkind responses crossed my mind. It's a good thing I kept my mouth shut! In my husband's defense, he was too groggy to notice I was crying. When I didn't get up off the floor very quickly, he came to my rescue. Better late than never?

I'm still rather pleased with myself for controlling my tongue. That's an area of constant struggle for me. My tongue slips far more often than my feet, and it has caused more serious injuries. Perhaps someday unkind thoughts won't even enter my head, but for now I'll be content if they don't exit my mouth!

■ Dear God, give me your strength to control my tongue. Guard my speech; don't let careless, unkind words slip out in my unguarded moments. Don't let me gossip, nag, complain, grumble, argue, or lie. Help me keep a tight rein on my tongue!

Do Not Follow the Crowd in Doing Wrong

"*Do not follow the crowd in doing wrong.*

Exodus 23:2

The tide of children ran in and out of the sanctuary after the service, while their parents nonchalantly visited. I recognized two small blonde heads bobbing in the midst of the tumult and promptly beached their bottoms on a pew. "Everybody's doing it, Mom!" came their protests.

"Not any more," I replied flatly. "*You're* not! You two somebodies know better."

Satan's rationalization takes root early, and the self-deception that goes with it often continues through the years. Here are some examples of faulty logic I've fallen privy to. "Everybody's going 65, why should I drive the speed limit?" "Everybody occasionally calls in sick just to get a day off. Why shouldn't I take a 'mental health' day?" "Everybody else will be wearing a new Easter outfit . . . and I do have a charge card!"

"Not everybody," God responds, taking me aside. "*You* know better!"

■ Lord, help me to realize the dangers of following the crowd. Mary would certainly have slighted her devotional life if she had gone along with the common practice, as Martha suggested. Keep my conscience sensitive, Lord, and give me courage to follow you rather than follow along with what "everybody's doing."

My Burden Is Light

"'Take my yoke upon you and learn from me, for I am gentle and humble in heart, and you will find rest for your souls. For my yoke is easy and my burden is light.'

Matthew 11:29-30

The words, "Mommy, I missed you today," followed by tiny arms squeezing your neck can certainly boost a mother's morale. It helps so much to know that somebody cares whether you're there or not. The knowledge that there are people close to you, and not only the little ones with sticky hands, but an entire family, who need you and love you is quite an inspiration to keep on striving to be a good mom.

Life in the mother's track is demanding and often fast-paced, but God did not mean for it to be a burden. God intends for it to be fulfilling and enjoyable, full of blessing. Breaks from the children and times of refreshment are needed to ease the temptation to give up or become weary of doing a good job. A habit of casting our cares upon the Lord is also essential.

Take time to learn from God. Take some time for yourself, and don't feel guilty. And just maybe you'll find the greeting you get when you return home is the best part of being away!

■ Lord, thank you for the privilege I have of being loved enough to be missed when I'm gone. Thank you for our family's love for one another. Please encourage me during the difficult times by showing me the rewards of sticking to the job. Thank you for the children I cherish and the joy they bring to my heart.

MARTHA SERVED

Martha Served

"*Jesus arrived at Bethany. . . . Here a dinner was given in Jesus' honor. Martha served, while Lazarus was among those reclining at the table with him. Then Mary took . . . perfume; she poured it on Jesus' feet and wiped his feet with her hair.*

John 12:1-3

In this story, Mary and Jesus were the lead characters. But let's look at someone in a supportive role—Martha.

The setting was the home of Simon the Leper (see Mark 14:3). Then why was Martha serving? Lazarus was a guest, reclining at the table with the Lord. Mary came in later with an alabaster jar of perfume. But "Martha served."

Apparently Martha had a reputation in Bethany for organizing and preparing large banquets with skill. She must have been asked to cater the meal. She was a talented hostess and used her abilities willingly to serve others. Martha was willing to work behind the scenes, out of the limelight. Yet what Mary did was not the only story told; Martha's performance was also noted! Sandwiched into the narrative are the words, "Martha served." What a tribute, to have your name recorded in God's Word for faithful service! Sometimes what appears to be menial service isn't really a "bit part." God must have thought it was worth recording.

■ Lord, I want to have a reputation for excellence in what I do. I want people to know that I can be counted on to do a good job. Help me be content to perform in the role that suits me best, the one you have chosen for me, even if it's not the "leading lady."

A Time to Laugh

"There is a time for everything, and a season for every activity under heaven . . . a time to weep and a time to laugh.

Ecclesiastes 3:1, 4

It's spring! The house is in shambles, as our toddler wants to be outside every waking, noneating moment. And when Evan's outside, so am I.

I guess I should count my blessings. Last year he was in the "most bugs are edible" stage of development, which required even greater surveillance! This year only his constant climbing is hazardous.

Today I tried to slip inside to straighten up. It didn't pay. While I was inside, Evan busied himself making tomato mulch out of the petunias. I wouldn't have minded so much if he hadn't tiptoed down the row of begonias yesterday! I have a few more flowers to plant, but between the dog and the kids I think it would be wiser to let them die peacefully in the box.

Am I the only one who occasionally finds keeping house and loving kids at odds with one another?

When I stayed outside with Evan, the others sneaked in from the sandbox and poured their own lemonade. . . . Now I probably should have praised their self-sufficiency, but the gritty floor and napkin-laminated tabletop they left behind made it hard for me to keep a positive attitude (especially when my husband found the whole thing amusing!).

It's beneath my sense of dignity to admit defeat so early in the season, so I'm left with only one alternative: to laugh at this ridiculous mess they've gotten me into! (And spray the sticky little culprits with the garden hose—I generally win one-sided water fights!)

■ Father, thank you for a husband and kids who can see the humor in things. Help me appreciate it and develop my own sense of humor instead of thinking, "Sure you think it's funny. *You* don't have to clean up the mess!" Teach me to laugh easily and often. Don't let me take things too seriously. There is no use in crying over spilled lemonade!

"Marital Duty"

"*The husband should fulfill his marital duty to his wife, and likewise the wife to her husband.*

1 Corinthians 7:3

In the hush at the close of the day, their eyes meet. They move toward their bedroom where she lights a candle, and they "slip into something a little more comfortable." He puts on soft music. They dance. He kisses her gently, then more intently. . . .

The sound of little feet running down the hall warns them only seconds before an excited two-year-old bursts through the door. "Daddy! Mommy! I hear music!" he exclaims, his eyes sparkling with interest.

She dives for the sheets. He darts for the door. "It's time for you to be in bed, son," he announces as he whisks the child up in his arms and carries him back down the hall.

The little boy protests loudly as he strains to peek over his father's shoulder, "But, Daddy, I hear music!"

If it's ever happened to you, you know that it's not always easy to "fulfill your marital duty" once you have children! If you've ever taken family vacations, you also know that motel accommodations present the ultimate challenge. By the time you have taken care of all the distractions and interruptions, the answer to "Now, where were we?" may be "Who cares!" And what are vacations for!

But even if the scheme to work in a rendezvous fails, there's a special closeness in being coconspirators. It's a playful sense of camaraderie that comes from trying to sneak one past the children!

The normal companionship of parents raising their family, and the confidential conversations and concerns they share, can reinforce the intimacy which finds natural expression in sexual fulfillment. But incompatible schedules, lack of romance, and fatigue can threaten to diminish any couple's love life.

Intimacy in marriage, at all levels, must be carefully nurtured. Barbara Rainey, who with her husband has coauthored two books on marriage, suggests, "As wives, let's cherish our privileged responsibility and protect our men in the areas where they struggle. In the physical realm especially, we need to be more enthusiastic and available." Time alone with our husbands should be carefully guarded.

So let there be music! (And locked doors!)

■ Father, thank you for the husband you have given me, and the intimacy you have designed for marriage. Help us spend more time adoring, admiring, and appreciating each other. Don't let us take our relationship for granted, but lead us to an ever-increasing knowledge of the oneness and pleasure of marital love.

There Is Freedom

“The Lord is the Spirit, and where the Spirit of the Lord is, there is freedom. And we, who with unveiled faces all reflect the Lord’s glory, are being transformed into his likeness with ever-increasing glory, which comes from the Lord, who is the Spirit.

2 Corinthians 3:17-18

Where the Spirit of the Lord is, there is freedom. We are free from the performance treadmill of attempting to be better Christians by doing more, learning more, earning more approval from God. We are released from the burden of trying to live up to our own unreachable expectations.

We are free to let up on ourselves, to humbly concede that we cannot do the things we ought to do. Instead of being self-reformed, we are Spirit-transformed! We can yield ourselves to God with complete and restful confidence that the Spirit is at work in us.

The Holy Spirit is God—not a yearning or an influence or tender feeling. The Spirit is indispensable. Trying to live out the life to which God calls us, without the power of the Spirit, is like trying to play music on an electric piano without plugging it in. It is the Spirit who brings us into harmony with God’s will and transforms us into the image of God.

The Holy Spirit lifts off the weight of performance-based acceptance. In the Spirit, we are at liberty to love and accept ourselves, and to feel God’s pleasure. By daily dependence on the Spirit, the God of grace can use us as we are, while we are becoming more Christlike.

■ Lord, help me to relinquish my depressing self-criticism, "I should do better. . ." and to praise you for your ongoing work in me. Help me find new dimensions of faith, joy, and blessing to others, through the work of your Spirit. Thank you for the present power of the Spirit, and for your healing grace.

A Neighbor's House

"*You shall not covet your neighbor's house . . . or anything that belongs to your neighbor.*

Exodus 20:17

Old farm houses are known to be drafty. One of our neighbors claims he can actually see his curtains move on gusty days. When the wind is from the south, we get whitecaps on the toilet!

Some things grow better with age. Other things fall apart. Our farm house has settled into old age so comfortably that we can spill milk anywhere in the kitchen and it runs like the Missouri River to the corner under the refrigerator.

Showers, central air, and square corners all came along after its time. Actually, I think square corners were already in existence a hundred years ago; the carpenter just didn't believe in them. He did believe in doors. There are eight doorways in the kitchen alone. They range in height from an even six feet to seven feet, one inch. (I just measured.)

A close friend just built a beautiful home, complete with all the modern conveniences, flashy architecture, and even flashier interior decorating. I asked her what she enjoyed most about the house. She replied modestly, listing such things as the automatic garage door opener, the shower in the utility room, dishwasher, etc.

"Well," I teased, "if anything ever quits working, let me know, and I'll show you how to live without it!"

■ All joking aside, Father, don't let me covet the prosperity or possessions others enjoy. Remove any trace of petty jealousy in me. Thank you for the comforts we have in our home. And thank you, too, for the luxuries we don't have; for doing without can bring forth creativity, ingenuity, and strength of character. Above all, thank you for making our home a haven of love.

He Sought His God and Worked Wholeheartedly

"*This is what Hezekiah did throughout Judah, doing what was good and right and faithful before the Lord his God. In everything that he undertook . . . he sought his God and worked wholeheartedly. And so he prospered.*

2 Chronicles 31:20-21

I walked out of the pantry holding a wooden puzzle in each hand. "Which one do you want?" I asked our two-year-old, holding out both for him to see. "Those two!" he exclaimed as he snatched both puzzles.

Not knowing which one he preferred, Cale dumped all the pieces of his two puzzles in a big pile and began to work on first one, then the other. It amused me to watch him sorting pieces, trying to match Big Bird and Mickey Mouse alternately.

As I watched his actions, it seemed like God was saying, "This is what you're doing." I was moving back and forth between Mary and Martha activities, trying to sort out the two. I couldn't decide which should come first—prayer or practical attempts to complete my work—so I attempted both together. The result? Interrupted prayer. Distracted activity.

I was struggling with the delicate balance of being and doing. I wanted to sit at the feet of Jesus and learn to be the person I was created to be. And I wanted dinner to be ready on time! With no sister in the house to cover for me, this presented a problem. I was impatient with the circumstances that made extended times of silence, solitude, and study impractical.

As I watched my son patiently work on his two puzzles, inspecting each piece with interest, my own impatience seemed in sharp contrast. Wasn't it God who had given me both puzzles to work on? God knew I needed to serve and seek him. What if I had been given the very responsibilities I resented in order to draw me to God?

As I thought about it, it dawned on me that the separation between "spiritual" activities and "worldly" activities was an artificial division. The contemplation of what God required, and the completion of the tasks he assigned were interlocking pieces of the same abundant life he pictured for me. Meeting Christ, like Mary, and meeting the practical needs of those around me, like Martha, were both acceptable in God's sight. And God could speak wherever he chose—in my prayer closet or in my daily experiences.

"I did it!" Cale exclaimed as he dropped the last piece into place. I, too, felt a sense of satisfaction in putting together a more complete picture of practical devotion. Seeking God and working wholeheartedly both have their place. The Mary and the Martha in me can live comfortably together!

■ My Lord, thank you for speaking to me through daily activities as simple as child's play. I ask you to preside over my life, in the practical responsibilities as well as in my essential need for prayer. Help me to find the unity of worship and work, of wholeheartedly seeking you and heartily serving you.

To Find Satisfaction in Toilsome Labor

"*Then I realized that it is good and proper for a man to eat and drink, and to find satisfaction in his toilsome labor under the sun during the few days of life God has given him—for this is his lot. Moreover, when God gives any man wealth and possessions, and enables him to enjoy them, to accept his lot and be happy in his work—this is a gift of God.*

Ecclesiastes 5:18-19

Why is it that the full grown man at the grocery check-out counter gets to carry out one paper sack (full of napkins, marshmallows, foam plates, and chips) while I am left with two squirming, 35-pound passengers, purse, and a tag-along toddler to manage? Some picnic! Luckily, I left one with Grandma.

Why is it that my husband often suggests we return early from our evening out, fearing that we might be expecting too much from our sitter, but routinely leaves me to longer shifts?

Why is it that my friends with a small family have a dishwasher, household help, and disposable diapers? My only dishwasher wears a farm cap, doesn't do counters, and operates about one day in five.

I know everybody has their own row to hoe, but why is it some people get to use *ride-on* roto-tillers? And why does it always look like there are more weeds in my row?

Then again, why is it I insist on entertaining Comparison at all? I know he is a thief. He steals away my contentment and robs me of job satisfaction. To accept my lot and be happy in my work—this is God's gift to me—Comparison snatches it from my hand. Every chance he gets!

Why is it I cooperate, just hand him the chance? When I remember his monotonous technique—always whispering petty thoughts about people better (not worse) off than I am—I should get smart to *whom* he works for.

■ Sovereign Lord, protect me. Take my eyes off others and put them back on you. Forgive me for comparing my work load with others and whining because they always seem to have it so easy. I don't know *their* lives. I am wrong to complain, to take for granted all your blessings, to overlook the many things you've done to make life easier for me.

Enable me to accept my lot and be happy in my work, trusting that you know what you're doing and that you don't make mistakes in choosing personnel or assigning their tasks. Help me to be diligent, thankful for the ability to carry out the work required, and grateful for the chance to serve a loving God.

God Teaches Us to Say No

"*It [the grace of God] teaches us to say "No" to ungodliness and worldly passions, and to live self-controlled, upright and godly lives in this present age.*

Titus 2:12

My son began spinning around and around and around in circles with his arms extended. When he saw me enter the room, he abruptly stopped and exclaimed, "Mommy, watch me spinning 'round and 'round; maybe I will get *busy*!"

Do you ever feel like you're running around in circles, getting busier and busier? Most of us mothers feel an innate obligation to say yes to church, community, social, and job-related activities until our heads spin. But instead of recognizing the problem, we often bow to the audience who applauds our efforts, "Look how *busy* she is! She does this and this and this and still has time to take care of her husband and kids."

But she doesn't. In reality she often collapses on the carpet in exhaustion when she finally gets home. And her kids spend a lot of time with his folks or at day care. And saying yes to outside activities has often resulted in saying no to her spouse, "Not tonight, dear, I'm too tired!"

Has God been teaching you to see overcommitment for what it is and what it results in—ungodliness? Overextending leads directly to ungodly behavior such as irritability, little time for prayer or Bible study, and failure to meet our family's need for loving attention. In the world of overcommitment, everyone *else* gets Mom's best effort while family members are squeezed into the remaining time slots because, "They'll understand just this once. . . ."

WEEK OF 3-23

Saying no to the worldly passions which prompt much of our activity is not easy. Our sinful nature craves achievement, public success, praise, money, and popularity. Even taking on "spiritual" commitments beyond what we can manage may result from worldly motives or an unwillingness to delay the gratification of our desires. We feel a sense of obligation, that we should say yes, and we feel guilt if we don't. Therefore, we must fight our natural bent toward excessive involvement wherever it surfaces. Too much of a good thing is *not* a good thing. And busyness is *not* next to godliness!

■ Lord, I'm not experiencing burnout yet, but things are getting a little bit toasty! I commit my schedule to you, asking you to guide my choices. It's so easy to crowd you out of my life. Help me to reserve strength, emotional energy, and time for my family, too, by saying a firm *no!* to overcommitment.

Let Your Gentleness Be Evident

"*Let your gentleness be evident to all.*

Philippians 4:5

There was only one question on the multiple choice test. But it was one of the hardest tests I've taken. See how well you score:

1) Today my gentleness was evident to
   A. My husband
   B. My children
   C. My friends
   D. None of the above
   E. All of the above

Does the evidence in your life prove you to be a gentle person? Before you answer, consider these synonyms for gentleness: calmness, kindness, tolerance, consideration, courtesy. Or, in rushed moments do you find yourself using a harsh tone of voice, losing your temper, or acting out of frustration or impatience?

If you see room for improvement you may find that removing time pressure from daily activities, lowering the noise and confusion level by eliminating long hours of TV or radio, and adding a large dose of the great outdoors is the "homework" needed to pass the test.

■ Father, most days I'd rather not test myself against the standards set in your Word! Thank you that I am making progress in this area. Thank you for your Spirit who has produced fruit in me. I know I can't be shoved into being gentle; it takes time. Please help me continue to make time for gentleness, and thank you for being patient with me!

Mary Has Chosen What Is Better

"*'Mary has chosen what is better, and it will not be taken away from her.'*

Luke 10:42

When I first read this story, I greatly admired Mary. I wished to be more like her. While writing this book, I read and reread this passage. Quietly, over many days, there emerged a new knowledge of myself. I found myself to be a curious mixture of both Mary and Martha. Moreover, I began to feel that the blend was healthy, in fact, necessary.

At the time when these thoughts were coming together, I read the book *God's Joyful Surprise: Finding Yourself Loved* by Sue Monk Kidd. Toward the end of the book the author shared her experience during a retreat. The words seemed to jump off the page as I read:

"I'd come here to be with God, to listen to Him and experience His presence. But already I was making lists of activities to keep me busy. I was like Martha in the Bible who worked in the kitchen for Jesus while her sister Mary sat at his feet. I was back to the old struggle between inward movement and outward movement, between being and doing, between prayer and involvement. I had been a Martha all my life, with all my activities for God. Was there a Mary inside me? . . .

"I've learned since then that it is really wrong to separate the inner movement toward God in prayer from the outward movement toward God in ministry. They are meant to be intertwined and balanced in a way that makes them inseparable. We are called to be both Mary and Martha together. One without the other is to miss the point. But I am convinced that our 'Marthahood,' our involvement with a needy world, must flow like a byproduct from our contemplation at the feet of Jesus. It is the Mary in us that must form the core of all we do" (Harper & Row, 1987).

As I read these words, I felt a keen sense of exhilaration and a hush of worship. I was onto something! In the private corners of *my* heart God had revealed the truth, and was now reaffirming my fresh understanding through the words written by someone else who sought him. I laughed at the thought that our library had ordered the book "by mistake," and a friend who noticed it there "just happened" to mention it to me!

God *will* make himself heard, if we, like Mary, will listen! God speaks truth today when we study the Bible, when we respond in ministry, when we interact with those around us, and when we experience God's creation. We must learn to listen in many ways. God is creative enough to communicate clearly, even in the midst of a Martha's world!

■ You are awesome, O God, in your unfailing love and faithful guidance! Thank you for pointing out the Mary in me—and the Martha. Help me as a woman, a wife, and a mother to be all you created *me* to be. I am here to sit at your feet. Teach me!